This book of **Doodles** belongs to:

_____

Doodle your own self-portrait.

Book design: Charla Pettingill

Illustration assistant extraordinaire: Elizabeth Kidder

First Edition

ISBN: 978-1-938093-14-2

Printed in China

CPSIA Compliance Information: Batch #041513DP
For further information contact Duo Press, LLC at info@duopressbooks.com

duopress
www.duopressbooks.com

DOODLE AMERICA

By Jerome Pohlen • Illustrations by Violet Lemay

duopress

Doodle clouds and a big sun over this **imaginary** skyline of the United States.

Do you recognize some of these buildings?

• The Northeast

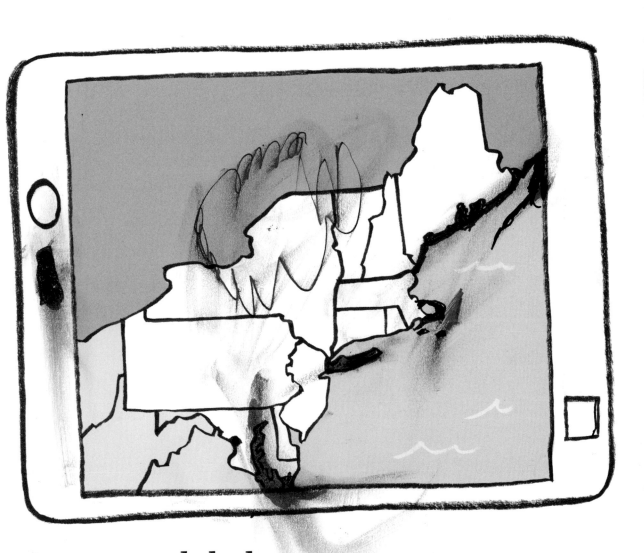

Can you **label** the states and Washington, D.C.?
*Connecticut * Delaware * Maine * Maryland * Massachusetts
* New Hampshire * New Jersey * New York * Pennsylvania
* Rhode Island * Vermont *

It's the Fourth of July—time for a parade! Doodle it.

America declared its independence on July 4, 1776.

Can you doodle stars and stripes on the flag?

Betsy Ross is said to have sewn the first American flag.

Doodle your own design for an American flag.

Who is in the **Oval Office?**

Every president except George Washington
has lived in the White House.

What is the **Statue of Liberty** holding in her hand?
Doodle it!

The Statue of Liberty was a gift from France.

What is happening on the boardwalk? Doodle it!

Many towns in New Jersey have boardwalks along the beach.

Doodle some spots on this cow.

Vermont is famous for its dairy farms.

Doodle a sunrise over the ocean.

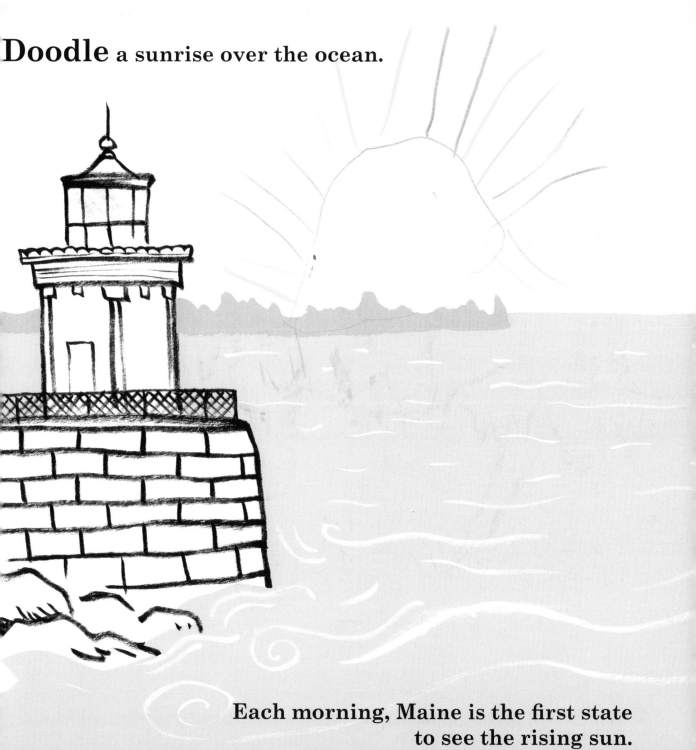

Each morning, Maine is the first state
to see the rising sun.

Can you **doodle** a turkey?

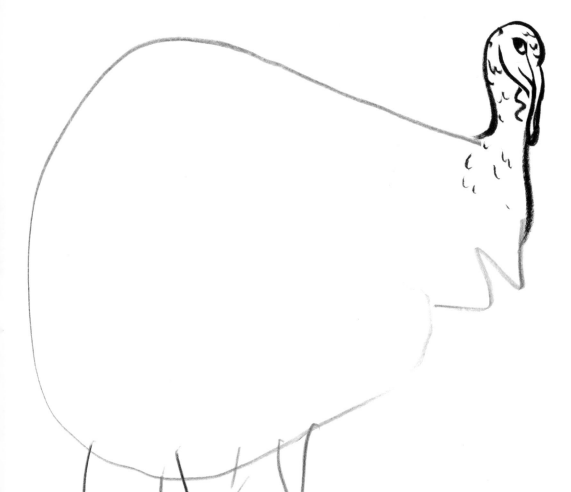

Ben Franklin wanted the turkey to be the national bird.

Who is running for president?

Every presidential campaign starts with the
New Hampshire primary.

What would you write in the **Constitution?**

We the People

Delaware was the first state to adopt the U.S. Constitution.

It's a three-ring circus! Who is performing?
Doodle them!

Circus fans can visit the Barnum Museum in
Bridgeport, Connecticut.

Doodle a **Thanksgiving** feast!

The first Thanksgiving was celebrated in
Plymouth, Massachusetts.

This buggy needs a horse. Doodle it!

Many Amish people live in central Pennsylvania.

Doodle Niagara Falls.

Which two teams would you like to see play in the World Series?

The Baseball Hall of Fame is in Cooperstown, New York.

The **Liberty Bell** is missing its crack. **Doodle it!**

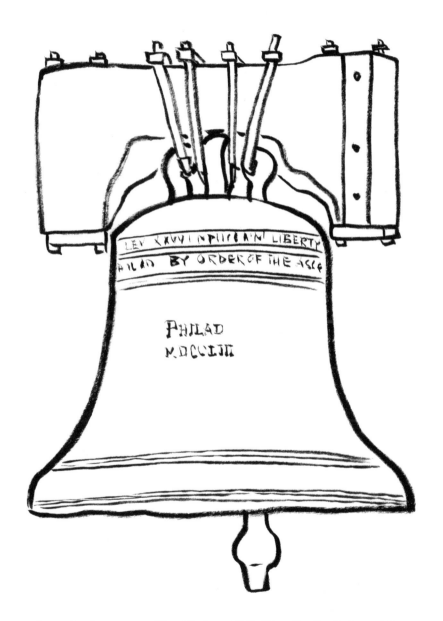

You can see the Liberty Bell in Philadelphia, Pennsylvania.

Doodle a lighthouse.

There are 63 lighthouses along the coast of Maine.

What did the fishermen catch?

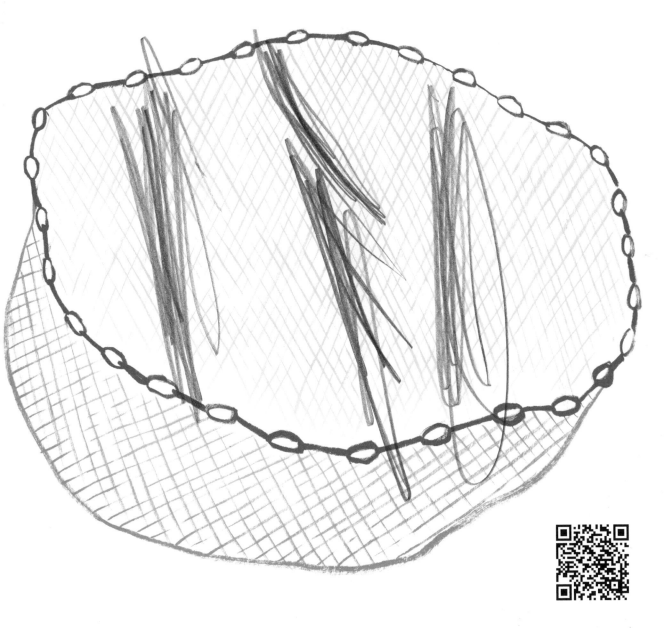

Scan this and get more fish and other
sea animals to doodle!

Who is playing basketball?

Basketball was invented in
Springfield, Massachusetts, in 1891.

Now **design** these two sneakers to wear for your next game.

The autumn leaves are turning —
color them, and draw even more.

Benjamin Franklin is flying a kite. Doodle it!

Doodle **fireworks** over **Baltimore Harbor.**

What has the farmer planted?

New Jersey is known as the Garden State.

The Redcoats are coming! The Redcoats are coming!
Doodle Paul Revere on his horse.

Draw some sailors on the **deck** of this ship.

The U.S. Naval Academy is located in Annapolis, Maryland.

This ship **needs** sails. **Doodle them!**

The USS *Constitution*—"Old Ironsides"—is docked in Boston Harbor.

Can you turn a can of soup into a work of art? Try it!

You can visit the Andy Warhol Museum in Pittsburgh, Pennsylvania.

Doodle the paintings from your **favorite** museum.

Doodle a spooky graveyard.

Edgar Allan Poe is buried in Baltimore, Maryland.

What will your next Halloween costume be? **Draw it!**

The muscleman **needs** tattoos.

What is the **weirdest thing** you've ever seen n your **hometown?**

Doodle wooden animals on the **carousel.**

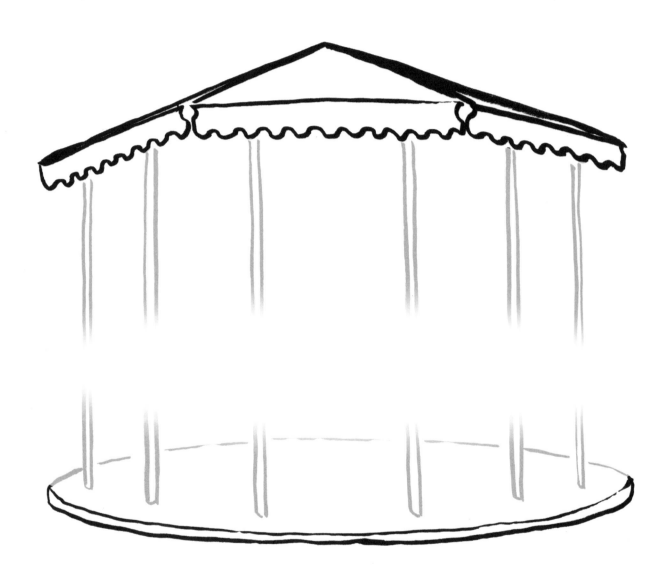

The Flying Horse Carousel in Watch Hill, Rhode Island, is America's oldest merry-go-round.

Doodle a **lobster** in this trap.

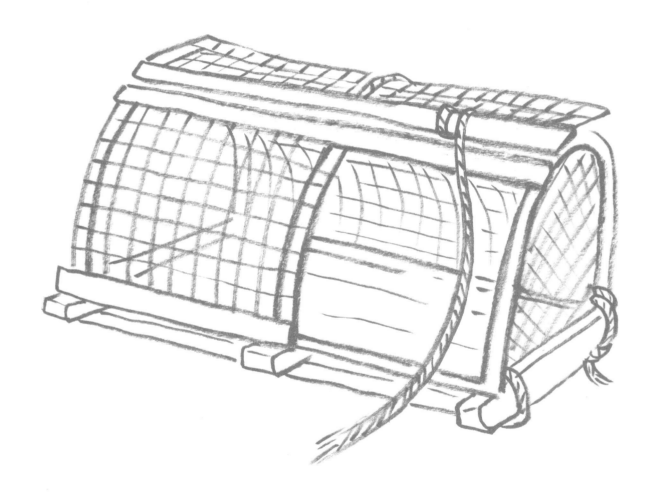

Are you a Yankee-Doodle?
Draw yourself riding to town on a pony.

. . . and don't forget to put a feather in your hat!

The South

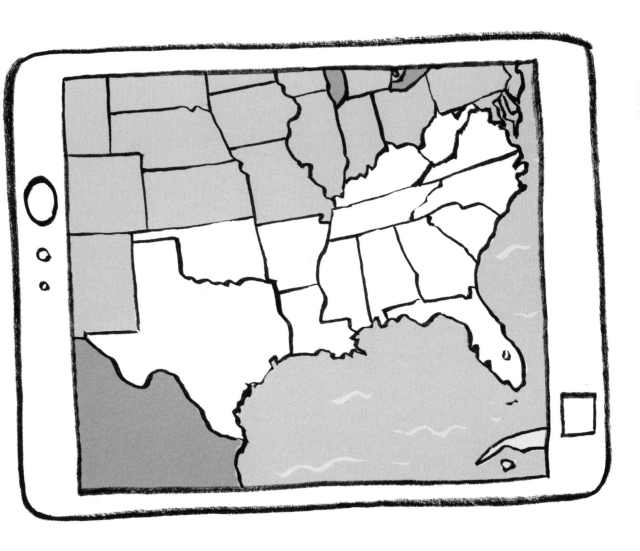

Can you **label** the states?
*Alabama * Arkansas * Florida * Georgia * Kentucky * Louisiana
* Mississippi * North Carolina * Oklahoma * South Carolina
* Tennessee * Texas * Virginia * West Virginia

Do you see any **alligators** in the swamp?
Doodle some more alligators!

Who is seated on the bus?

In 1955, Rosa Parks refused to give up her bus seat in Montgomery, Alabama.

Finish the Wright brothers' flyer.

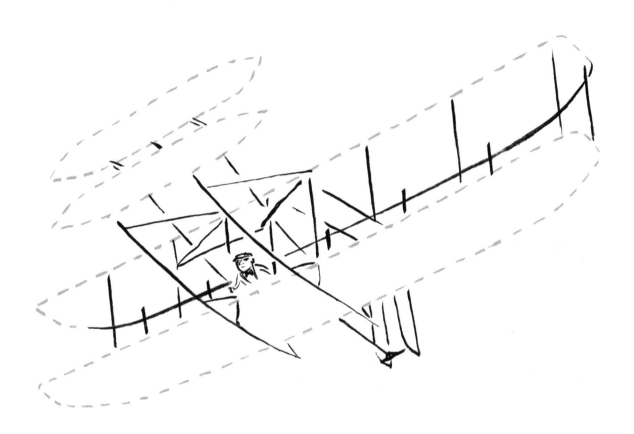

The Wrights made their first flight at Kitty Hawk, North Carolina.

Who is winning the Kentucky Derby?

This famous horse race has been held every spring since 1875.

Doodle some crazy Kentucky Derby hats.

Want to doodle more crazy hats? Scan this code!

Doodle some ducks in the fountain at the **Peabody Hotel.**

A family of ducks lives at this Memphis, Tennessee, hotel.

Time to take the dog for a walk!
Doodle your favorite pooch.

What is going on at the swimming pool?

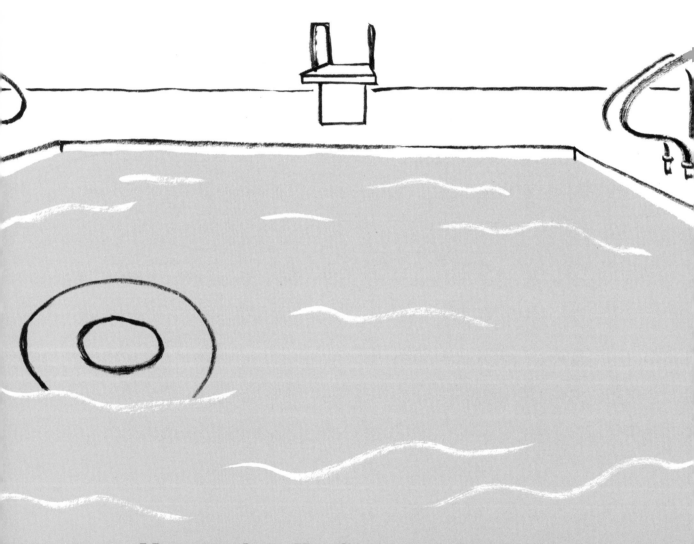

Many pools in Hot Springs, Arkansas, are heated by water from the earth.

What is your **favorite** ride at the carnival? **Doodle it!**

Who is singing at the Grand Ole Opry?

GRANDOLE

The Grand Ole Opry is broadcast from Nashville, Tennessee.

What **book** would you write about America? **Doodle a cover!**

Doodle the Mardi Gras Parade in New Orleans, Louisiana!

Mardi Gras is French for "Fat Tuesday."

The countdown has begun!
Doodle a rocket on the launching pad.

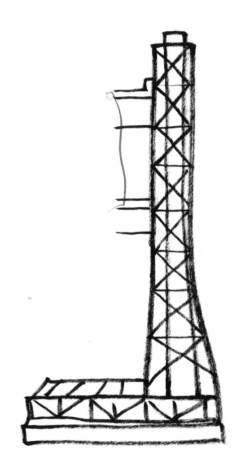

Future astronauts can visit the Kennedy Space Center in Florida.

Design a license plate for a car from your **favorite state.**

The kudzu is growing EVERYWHERE! Doodle it!

Kudzu is a vine that was brought from Japan to the South in 1876.

What is growing in the gardens?

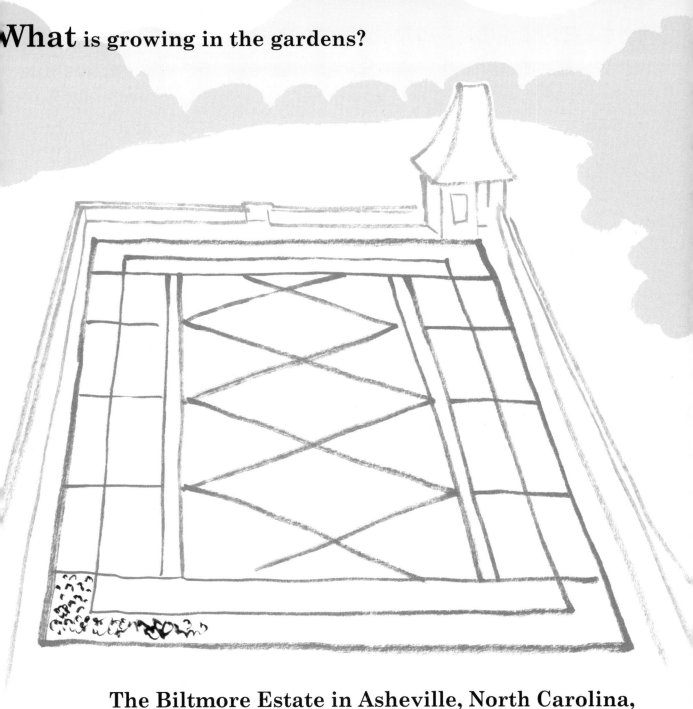

The Biltmore Estate in Asheville, North Carolina, has 75 acres of gardens.

What did you see at the **Civil War** reenactment?

The Civil War was fought from 1861 to 1865.

This monster truck needs some
BIG wheels—doodle them!

What is the juggler juggling? **Doodle it!**

People and performers say good-bye to the setting sun each night in Key West, Florida.

Who is riding in the carriage?

You can ride horse-drawn carriages in Charleston, South Carolina.

Doodle George and Martha Washington.

The Washingtons lived at Mount Vernon in northern Virginia.

What did you see at the zoo?

It's a yard sale! **What** did you find?

Doodle a **CRAZY** miniature golf course.

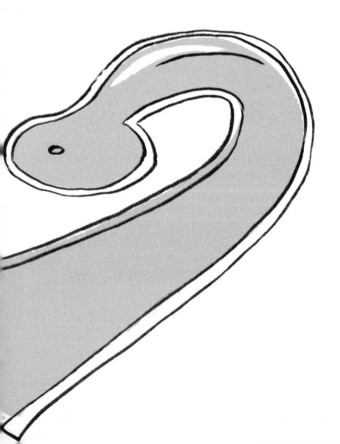

The first U.S. miniature golf course was built in Pinehurst, North Carolina.

Doodle a statue for the courthouse lawn.

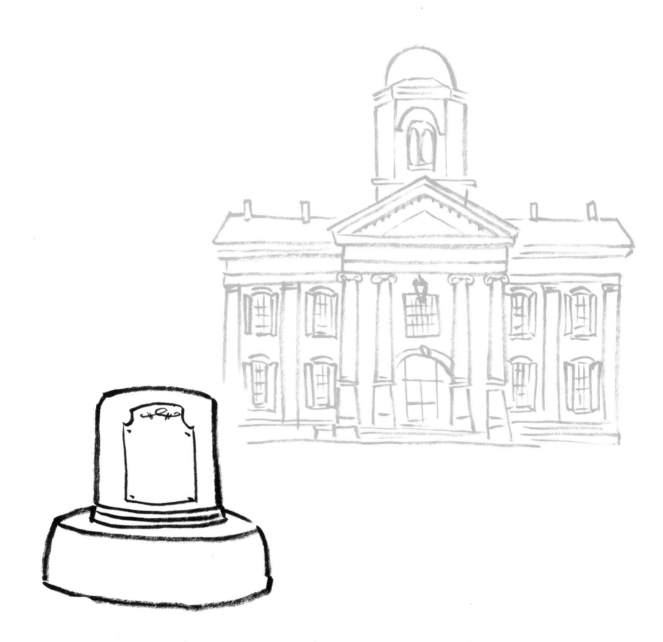

Decorate these drums.

There are 39 Native American tribes in Oklahoma.

Fill this fountain with green water
for St. Patrick's Day!

The largest fountain in Savannah, GA, is in Forsyth Park.

Martin Luther King Jr. said that he had a dream for America.
What is your dream?

Dr. King was born in Atlanta, Georgia, in 1929.

Who is parachuting? Doodle them!

There are bears in the woods! Doodle them!

About 1,500 black bears live in Great Smoky Mountains National Park.

Finish the Mississippi riverboat.
You can **color** it when you are finished!

What is the artist painting?
What would you paint on the other canvas?

The horse needs a saddle, bridle, and rider.
Doodle them!

What did you give for Mother's Day?

Mother's Day was first celebrated in Grafton, West Virginia.

Where are the balloons? **Doodle them!**

Most of America's helium comes from the ground beneath Amarillo, Texas.

Doodle some mermaids.

You can watch a mermaid show at
Weeki Wachee Springs in Florida.

Who is rocking on the porch?

• The Midwest and the Great Plains

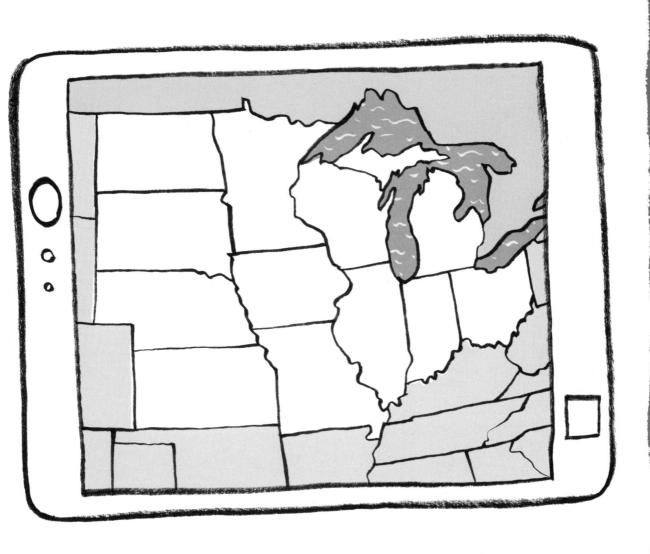

Can you **label** the states?

llinois * Indiana * Iowa * Kansas * Michigan * Minnesota * Missouri
* Nebraska * North Dakota * Ohio * South Dakota * Wisconsin

The **wagon train** is heading west—**draw it!**

The Oregon Trail passed Chimney Rock in Nebraska.

Abraham Lincoln is missing his hat. **Doodle it!**

Illinois is nicknamed the Land of Lincoln.

Whose faces would you put on Mount Rushmore?

Mount Rushmore is in the Black Hills of South Dakota.

Finish the sunflower.

Kansas is known as the Sunflower State.

What band is playing?

The Rock and Roll Hall of Fame is in Cleveland, Ohio.

Finish the bridge!

The Mackinac Bridge connects Michigan's two peninsulas.

Oh, give me a home, where the **buffalo** roam!
Doodle some buffalo!

You can still see herds of buffalo in North Dakota.

Which two teams would you like to see play in the Super Bowl?

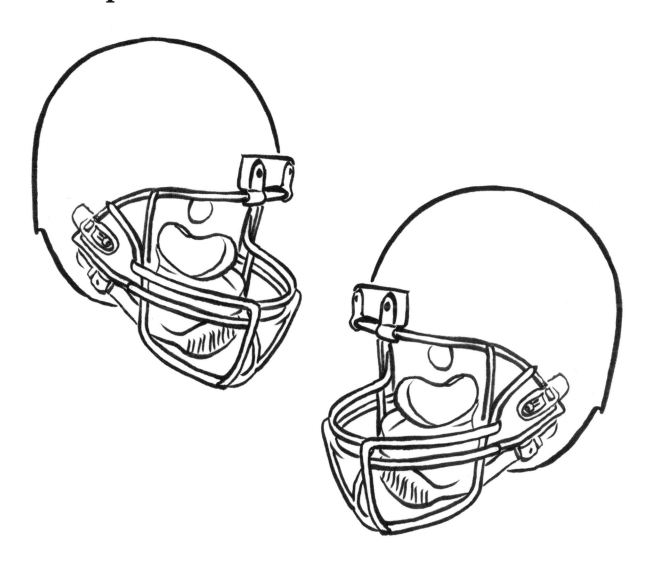

Football fans can visit the Pro Football Hall of Fame in Canton, Ohio.

What food did you eat at the state fair?

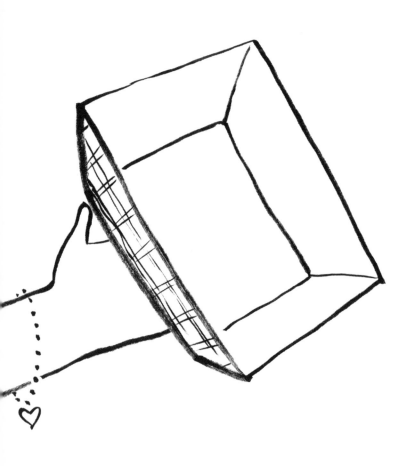

Finish the butter cow.

Every summer you can see a cow sculpted from 600 pounds of butter at the Iowa State Fair.

Color the dancers at the **powwow,** and draw some more!

Native Americans celebrate their culture with powwows.

What do the billboards say?

Who is canoeing on the lake?

There are 14,215 lakes in Minnesota.

What would you cook at a barbeque?

Kansas City is famous for its barbeque.

What is **your favorite** place to visit in your hometown? **Draw it!**

Who won the race?

The Indy 500 is held on Memorial Day weekend in Indianapolis, Indiana.

The Gateway Arch is missing! Doodle it.

The arch in St. Louis, Missouri, is the tallest monument in the United States.

What animals did you see at the farm?

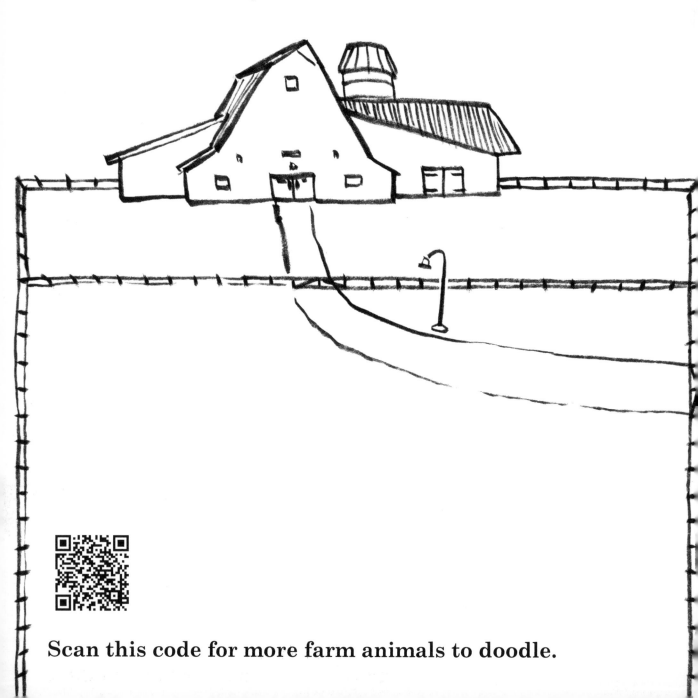

Scan this code for more farm animals to doodle.

Here's one **windmill**, but there's room for more.
Doodle them!

On the Great Plains, many farmers "grow" electricity on their land.

Fill the cave with stalactites and stalagmites.

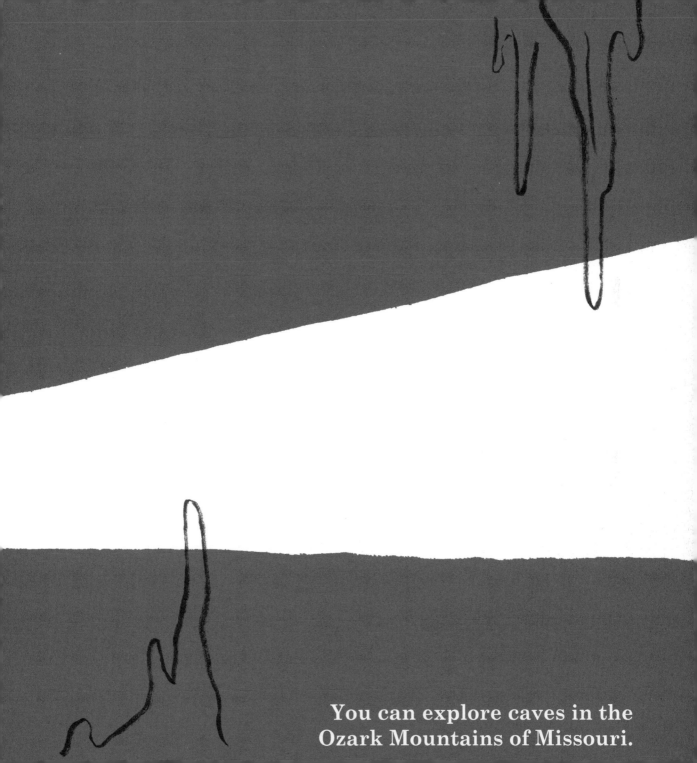

You can explore caves in the
Ozark Mountains of Missouri.

Time to **plant** a tree!

The very first Arbor Day was celebrated in Nebraska in 1872.

Doodle the tallest building you've ever seen.

Chicago, Illinois, has some of the tallest buildings in the United States.

Doodle your favorite team's uniforms on these players.

Indiana is famous for its
high school basketball championships.

What souvenirs did you buy on your trip?
Doodle them!

What would you wear to support your team?
Doodle it!

Some fans of the Green Bay Packers wear foam "Cheeseheads."

Pizza! Hot dogs!
What would YOU order for lunch in **Chicago?**

Doodle a **WILD** roller coaster!

**Ohio's Cedar Point amusement park
has 16 roller coasters!**

It snowed!
What are you going to do to enjoy the day?

Some Minnesota towns get over 70 inches of snow each year.

If you could design an **art museum,**
what would it look like?

**Some think the Milwaukee Art Museum
in Wisconsin looks like a bird.**

Can you **decorate** the **Corn Palace?**

The Corn Palace in Mitchell, South Dakota, has murals made of corn.

What new cars did you see at the auto show?
Doodle them!

Car companies show off their new models
at the Detroit Auto Show.

What artwork would you create for the Minneapolis Sculpture Garden?

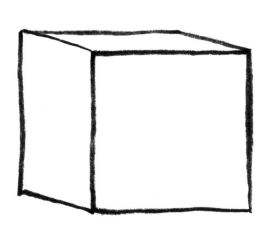

The *Spoonbridge and Cherry* sculpture was made by Claes Oldenburg and Coosje van Bruggen.

This famous painting is titled *American Gothic.*
Can you **doodle** your own masterpiece?

American Gothic was painted by
Iowa artist Grant Wood.

Doodle a CRAZY waterslide!

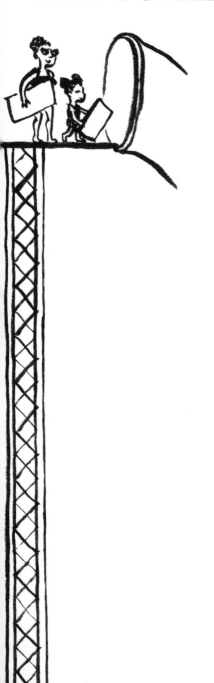

**The Wisconsin Dells calls itself the
Waterpark Capital of the World.**

What **bumper stickers** have you collected on vacation?

The West

Can you **label** the states?
* Alaska * Arizona * California * Colorado * Hawai'i * Idaho
* Montana * Nevada * New Mexico * Oregon * Utah
* Washington * Wyoming

What did you see in the desert? Doodle it!

This bucking bull needs a rider and horns!
Doodle them!

Cheyenne Frontier Days in Wyoming is one of the largest rodeos in the world.

Surf's up! Doodle some surfers.

The **Space Needle** is missing its top.
Doodle it!

Seattle's Space Needle was built for the 1962 World's Fair.

Doodle and color some tropical flowers.

The hibiscus is the state flower of Hawai'i.

Finish the other half of the Salt Lake Temple.

This famous building in Salt Lake City, Utah, took 40 years to build.

Doodle some rock climbers.

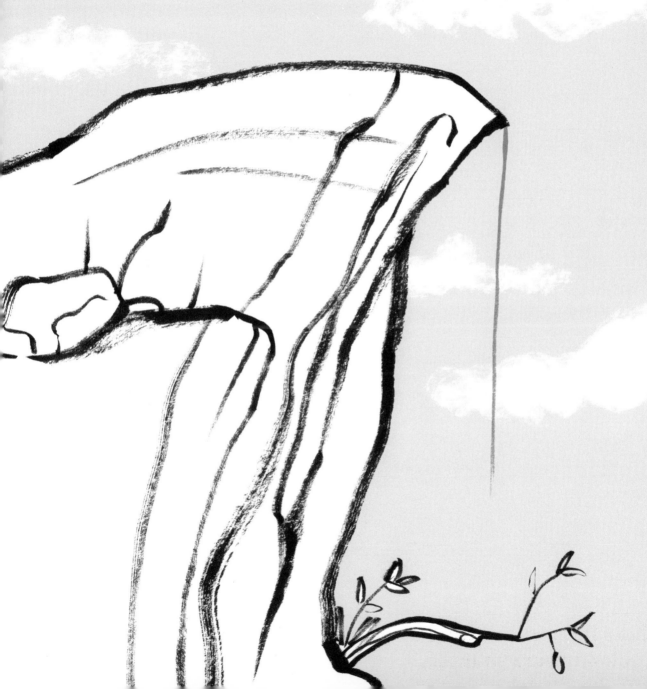

What did the paleontologist dig up?

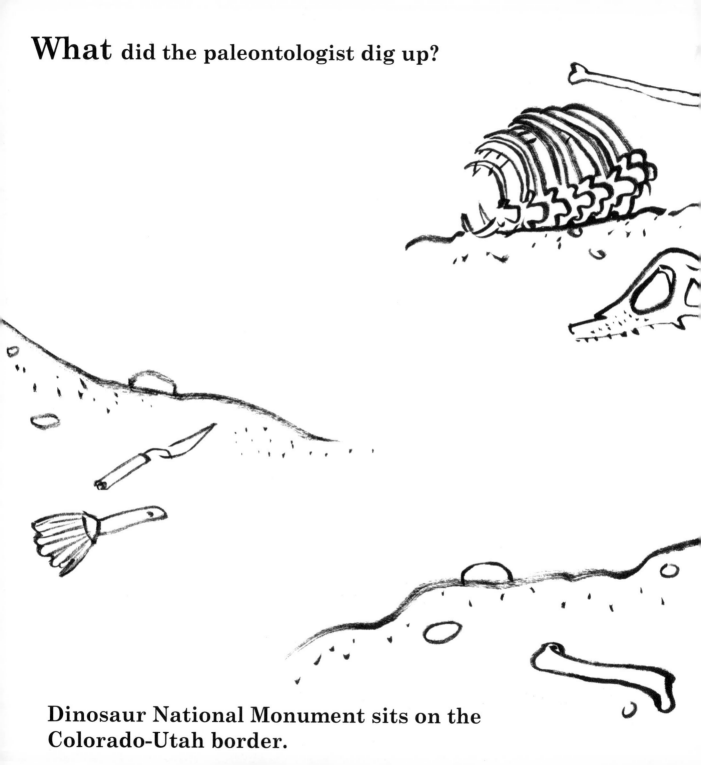

Dinosaur National Monument sits on the Colorado-Utah border.

Who has landed in the **flying saucer?**

**Every year Roswell, New Mexico,
throws a UFO Festival.**

Lights! Camera! Action!
What movie is being filmed?

Have you ever seen a movie set?

What will you pack for your vacation?
Doodle it!

What are the mules carrying on their backs?

There are no roads into Arizona's Grand Canyon—you have to hike or travel by horse or mule.

Doodle some skiers and snowboarders.

Colorado calls itself Ski Country USA.

The **geyser** is erupting—**doodle** it!

See the Old Faithful geyser in
Yellowstone National Park in Wyoming.

Have you seen the northern lights?
Doodle them!

The northern lights are usually bright green, but they can also be red.

Doodle some rock formations.

Utah's Bryce Canyon National Park
has strange rock formations.

The totem poles **need faces.**

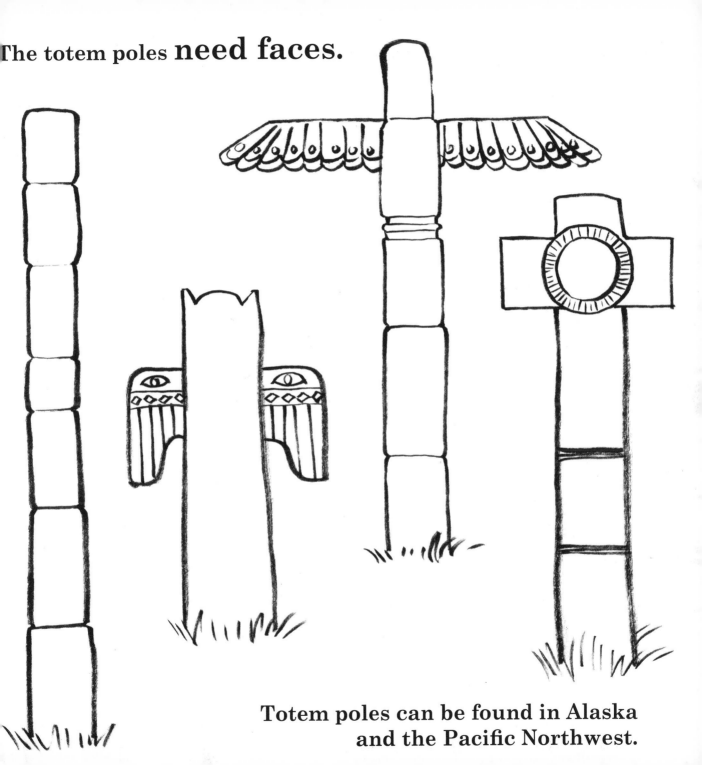

Totem poles can be found in Alaska
and the Pacific Northwest.

These people need **funny** sunglasses.

Who's at the beach?

These buildings need lights—LOTS of lights!

Fremont Street in Las Vegas, Nevada,
is famous for its neon lights.

Doodle patterns on the pottery.

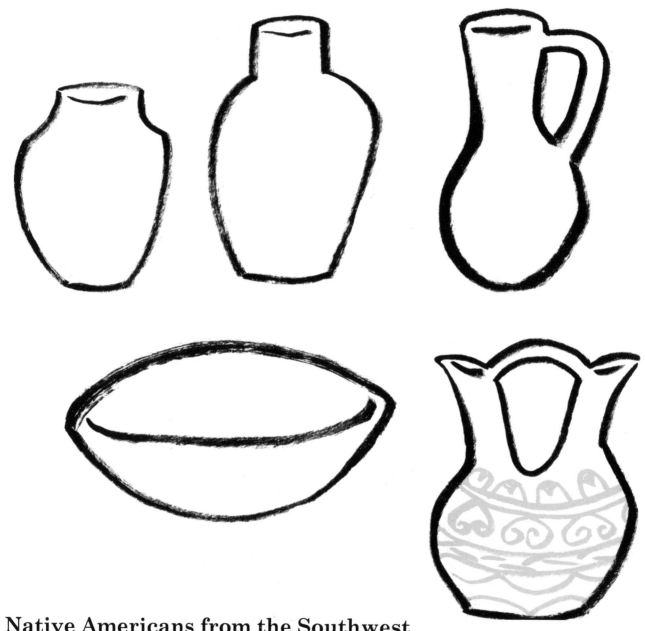

Native Americans from the Southwest are known for their pottery.

Who is sitting around the **campfire**?

What can you see from the top of Pikes Peak?
Draw it!

Katharine Lee Bates wrote "America the Beautiful" after climbing this Colorado mountain.

Do you like sushi? **Doodle it!**

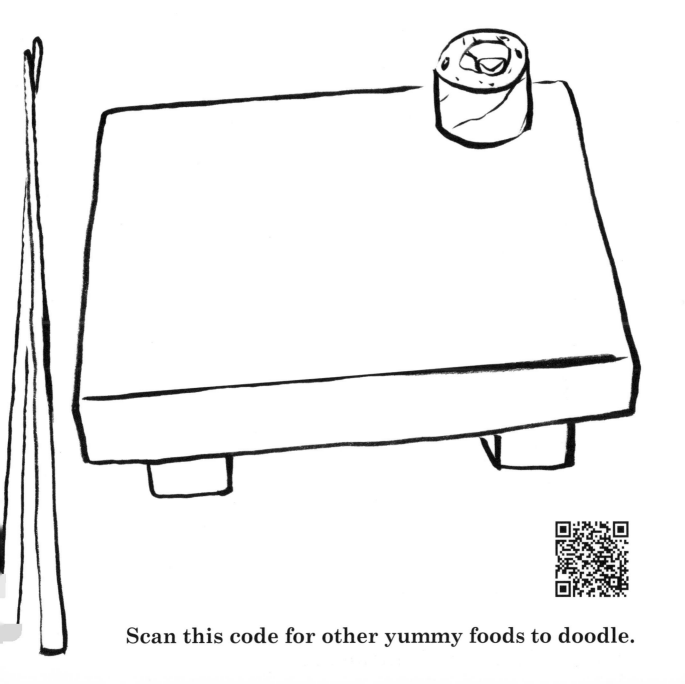

Scan this code for other yummy foods to doodle.

What is the STRANGEST thing you've ever seen on vacation? Draw it!

Doodle some hula dancers.

Have you ever been to a luau?

Doodle some clouds. What shapes do you see?

Montana is known as Big Sky Country.

Doodle some hang gliders.

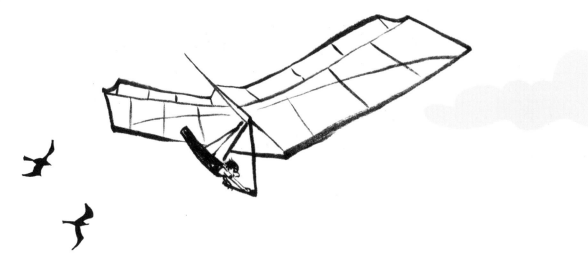

Hang gliding is a popular sport
along the California coast.

What's happening at the old ghost town?

Was that **Bigfoot?** Or just a bear?
Doodle what you saw in the forest.

Who is hiking in the mountains?

What is your favorite Tex-Mex food?
Doodle it on the plate.

This potato **needs** a face!

Idaho is famous for its potatoes.

Finish the parade float, then design your own!

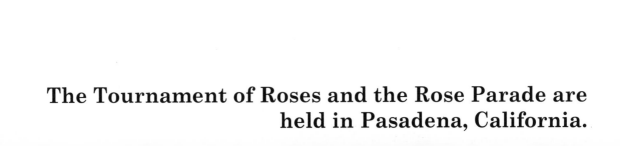

The Tournament of Roses and the Rose Parade are
held in Pasadena, California.

Doodle some animals on Seal Rock.

Many of the mammals you see along the Oregon coast are sea lions, not seals.

Doodle a hot-air balloon going up, up, and away!

Fill your **scrapbook** with photos of America.

How would you **draw** the state borders?